**◼◼ SCHOLASTIC**

# MATH Word Problems Made Easy

## Grade 5

### by Jill Safro

NEW YORK • TORONTO • LONDON • AUCKLAND • SYDNEY
MEXICO CITY • NEW DELHI • HONG KONG • BUENOS AIRES

**Teaching** *Resources*

Cover design by Maria Lilja
Interior design by Holly Grundon
Interior illustrations by Mike Moran

ISBN 0-439-52973-5
Copyright © 2005 by Jill Safro
All rights reserved.
Printed in the U.S.A.

4 5 6 7 8 9 10    40    12 11 10

# CONTENTS

# INTRODUCTION

**W**hen it comes to ranking math skills, problem solving is on top of the list. Literally. It's number one on the process standards listed in the *Principles and Standards for School Mathematics* (NCTM, 2000). According to the National Council of Teachers of Mathematics (NCTM), *"Problem-solving should be the central focus of all mathematics instruction and an integral part of all mathematical activity."* In other words, problem solving is what math is all about.

When learning to read, we learn to recognize the letters of the alphabet, we practice letter–sound relationships, and we learn punctuation. But the goal is to eventually read text. The same goes for math. We learn how to recognize and write numerals, decipher symbols, determine numerical order, and work with operations like addition and subtraction. But what matters most is what we can do with these skills—applying what we know to solve problems in daily life.

*Math Word Problems Made Easy: Grade 5* is designed to help you help students sharpen their problem-solving abilities (and share a chuckle or two along the way). This book is divided into three main sections to help you:

## The Fantastic Five-Step Process

**T**he first section describes a simple five-step problem-solving process and an introductory lesson you can share with your students. This process can be used with every math word problem they might encounter. This is a valuable concept to introduce at the beginning of the year and practice with students so that they will have an approach they can rely on as they encounter various types of problems throughout the year.

## The Amazing Eight Strategies

**S**ection two takes a look at the different types of problems students might encounter and describes eight strategies to consider when solving them. We discuss each strategy and provide sample problems (and solutions) so students can practice and master the strategy. You may want to introduce a new strategy every week, so that students will be thoroughly familiar with all the basic strategies and have had practice with them by the end of the second month of the school year.

## The Happy Hundred Word Problems

**H**ere you'll find 100 word problems that focus on math concepts specific to fifth grade. They're all written so students will find them interesting and fun.

The problems are arranged by mathematical standards. There are sections for Number and Operations, Algebra, Geometry, Measurement, and Reasoning. The problems are printed two to a page, leaving plenty of room for students to show their thinking. Use the problems to introduce concepts, practice strategies, or as an end point to check for understanding.

**L**earning a consistent problem-solving approach, becoming familiar with and practicing effective problem-solving strategies, and applying these ideas in word-problem contexts help students become more effective problem solvers and mathematicians. And with *Math Word Problems Made Easy: Grade 5*, they just might enjoy themselves while doing so.

# The Fantastic Five-Step Process

**W**hat do you do when you first encounter a math word problem? This is what we need to help students deal with. We need to help them develop a process that they can use effectively to solve any type of math word problem. The Five-Step Process will help students *organize* their interpretation of and thinking about word problems.

The best way to help students understand the process is to demonstrate how to use it as you work through a problem on the board or overhead. Make a copy of the graphic organizer below. You can blow this up into a poster or provide each student with his or her own copy to refer back to as you bring students through this introductory lesson.

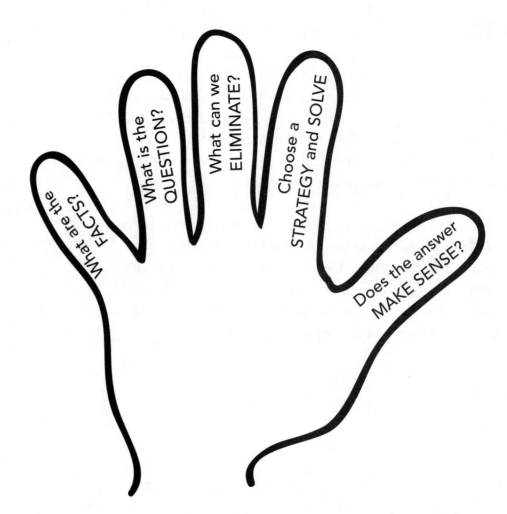

# Step 1: What Do We Know?

Begin by writing this problem on the board or overhead.

> Every year, Wienerville, Wisconsin, has a hot dog-eating contest. This year, there were four contestants. Little Frankie Footer ate 58 dogs. His brother Benny ate 3 times as many. Their friend, Phyllis, ate 180. Her brother Doug didn't eat any. Benny says he won the contest. Did he? How many dogs did he devour?

Read the problem carefully. What are the facts? Have students volunteer these orally. Write them on the board.

> Frankie Footer ate 58 hot dogs.
> Benny ate 3 times as many as Frankie.
> Phyllis ate 180 hot dogs.
> Doug didn't eat any.

Encourage students to write down the facts. This will help them focus on what is important while looking for ways to put it in a more accessible form. Can we arrange the facts in a way that will help us understand the problem situation? For instance, maybe it would be helpful to draw what we know, or put it in a list, or make a table. Sometimes it's helpful to arrange numbers from lower to higher or higher to lower, especially if we are asked to compare.

# Step 2: What Do We Want to Know?

What is the question in the problem? What are we trying to find out? It is a good idea to have students state the question and also determine how the answer will be labeled. For example, if the answer is 180, then 180 what? 180 pumpkins? 180 fish? In this case, it's hot dogs.

> We want to know two things:
> 1.  Did Benny win the contest?
> 2.  How many hot dogs did Benny eat?

## Step 3: What Can We Eliminate?

Once we know what we're trying to find out, we can decide what is unimportant. You may need all of the information, but usually there is some extra information that can be put aside.

> We can eliminate the fact that Doug didn't eat any hot dogs. Obviously he didn't win the contest.

## Step 4: Choose a Strategy or Action and Solve

Is there an action in the story (for example, something being taken away or shared) that will help decide on an operation or a way to solve the problem?

> Since we know that Benny ate 3 times as many as Frankie, we need to multiply Frankie's total (58) by 3:
>
> $$58 \times 3 = 174$$
>
> Benny ate 174 hot dogs! That's less than Phyllis's 180. He lost the contest, because 180 is a greater number than 174.

## Step 5: Does My Answer Make Sense?

Reread the problem. Look at the answer. Is it reasonable? Is it a sensible answer given what we know?

> It makes sense. 180 is higher than 174, and 174 is higher than 58. If the product was lower than 58, that would be a problem because the product of two positive numbers cannot be lower than the multiplicand.

Try a few different word problems using this "talk through" format with students. You can use sample problems from this book. Ask students to take a stab at the problem themselves first, and then do the step-by-step process together. Practicing the process in this way helps make it a part of a student's way of thinking mathematically.

# The Amazing Eight Strategies

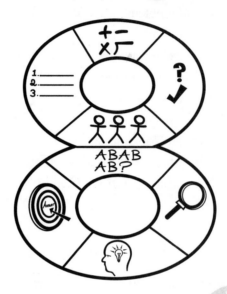

While we should encourage the use of the Five-Step Process to approach any problem, Step 4 (Choose a Strategy or Action and Solve) includes a wide range of choices. Some common strategies that are helpful to teach and practice are listed on the next few pages, along with sample problems. Students should have experience with all of the strategies. The more practice they have, the easier it is for them to choose a strategy that fits the problem and helps deliver an answer.

## Tip

As students learn about and practice using these strategies to solve problems, ask them to create their own word problems. You can list the math concepts you want them to use in the problems (such as multiplication or fractions) and even the strategy that must be used to solve it. Students use these parameters to create their own problems, which they can share and try out with one another. As students begin to play with these elements, their knowledge of how problems work grows, as does their confidence when encountering new problems.

# Choose an Operation

**CHOOSE AN OPERATION**

**E**ven the most straightforward problem requires a mathematical operation to solve it. The question is, which one? After examining the information presented in a problem, students must decide which operation (addition, subtraction, multiplication, or division) they should use to solve it. Instruct them to read the problem and look for key words and phrases, such as "all together" or "more than" that may help move them in the right direction when choosing an operation. Then have them write an actual equation and solve.

## SAMPLE PROBLEM

Uncle Otto ate a whole pumpkin pie in 21 minutes flat. Cousin Orville ate a whole pie in $\frac{1}{3}$ of that time. How long did it take Orville to eat the pie?

## Solution

Otto ate the pie in 21 minutes. Orville's time was $\frac{1}{3}$ of that. One operation we could use to figure out Orville's time is division. With the information in the problem, we can create an equation:

$$21 \div 3 = ?$$

**Answer:** It took Orville 7 minutes to eat the whole pie.

# SAMPLE PROBLEMS

**1.** Sylvia Snead won $500 on the new reality show *Who Wants to Do Howie's Homework*? She spent $25 on presents for her parents. She spent 3 times that amount on a purple poncho for her friend Paula. And she gave the rest to Howie. How much money did Sylvia give to Howie?

**2.** The Dingaling Brothers' Incredibly Brief Circus is in town. The Flying Frittata Brothers open the show with a 2-minute act. They are followed by Leo the Lion Tamer's 30-second performance. Finally, Tiny Tooley closes the show with a 90-second tightrope walk. How long was the show?

**3.** When Winnie the witch wiggles her nose, 70 radishes roll across the room. How many times must Winnie wiggle to make 1,190 radishes roll?

**4.** Rudy Rodin is sculpting the feet of the Quincy quintuplets. How many toes will Rudy make in all?

## ANSWERS

**1.** $400 (multiplication and subtraction)

**2.** 4 minutes (addition)

**3.** 17 times (division)

**4.** 50 toes (multiplication)

## STRATEGY 2:
# Guess & Check

**GUESS & CHECK**

**I**f you're not sure how to tackle a word problem, begin with a reasonable guess to get you started. Urge students to apply their estimation skills. This is the key to making a "reasonable" guess. Even just this first step is worth practicing. Then when a first attempted answer is arrived at, consider whether the answer is reasonable, too high, or too low. This is the "check" part of Guess and Check.

After considering the answer, have students decide if they need to revise and if so, how. Would a higher answer make sense? A lower answer? Try the following problem on the board and think aloud through the steps. Discuss the problem with students as you decide on your first attempt. Explain why you chose that number and how you are examining the number to determine if it is reasonable. Talk about how you are adjusting your initial attempt and why.

## SAMPLE PROBLEM

> Penelope Pig is eating her way through Cooter's Candy-Coated Bugs Shop. When she got there, there were two $5.25 chocolate-covered centipedes on the display shelf. There were also ten $2 caramel-coated spiders and six $1.50 cockroaches dipped in white chocolate. Penelope eats all but 3 of the candy-coated bugs. The 3 bugs are worth $8.25. What's left?

## Solution

According to the problem, Penelope ate all but $8.25 worth of bugs and only 3 bugs were left.

Let's say one of each kind of bug is left: $5.25 + $2 + 1.50 = $8.75. The sum is too high! It seems reasonable that one of the bugs left is the centipede ($5.25) because its price will get us close to the desired total. We know that the other two bugs must be the same kind. What would give us the difference between the $8.25 total and the $5.25 centipede?

Let's try the cockroaches: $5.25 + $1.50 + $1.50 = $8.25 The answer checks out. Penelope did not eat 1 centipede and 2 cockroaches.

# SAMPLE PROBLEMS

**1.** Shelly Shortbread is standing on her sister Susie's shoulders. Together, they're 48 inches tall. Shelly is 4 inches taller than Susie. How tall is Susie?

**2.** Magico the magician has 3 jars of invisible ink. Jar 2 has twice as much in as Jar 1. Jar 3 has twice as much as Jar 2. Together, the three jars hold 154 ounces of ink. How much ink is in each jar?

**3.** Dexter Donnelley has a massive molecule collection. He offers 18,473 molecules to his friend Frank. He offers another 16,849 molecules to his Aunt Evelyn. He offers 17,777 molecules to his neighbor Neville. And he offers 18,020 to Monty, the curator of the Museum of Molecules. Dexter ends up giving away 52,646 molecules. Who turned down his offer?

**4.** Quentin the cobbler makes orthopedic slippers for bats and cats. Today he made slippers for twice as many cats as bats. That's 130 individual slippers! How many bat slippers did he make?

## ANSWERS

**1.** 22 inches tall

**2.** Jar 1 has 22 ounces, Jar 2 has 44 ounces, and Jar 3 has 88 ounces.

**3.** Frank

**4.** 26 bat slippers

# Draw a Picture

DRAW A PICTURE

**D**rawing a picture can help answer the question, "What do we know?" Sometimes words do not easily convey the facts. Sometimes they can even confuse. By having students draw what they know, the problem can become clearer, the facts more easily manipulated, and relationships more quickly discovered.

When students use drawings or diagrams to help solve problems, remind them to use simple symbols to represent elements in a problem, such as stick figures for people. Unnecessary details or coloring should be left out.

## SAMPLE PROBLEM

If there's one thing the Frost family enjoys, it's building snowmen. Today, they built 12! They put black hats on half of the snowmen. One third of the snowmen got red hats. After that, the Frosts ran out of hats. So the rest are wearing wigs. How many snowmen are wearing wigs?

### Solution

**Answer:** 2 snowmen are wearing wigs

# SAMPLE PROBLEMS

**1.** Loneliville, Long Island, has 2 residents and they live 1,100 miles apart. (It's a very long island.) The Loneliville train stops at both of their houses. It also stops every 100 miles in between. How many stops does the train make?

**2.** Seymour sewed a brass button on each sleeve of his coat collection. He has 13 coats but 7 of them are missing one sleeve. How many buttons did Seymour sew?

**3.** Galinda guzzled $\frac{1}{17}$ of the guava juice in Gulliver's glass. Drew drank 6 times the amount that Galinda did. Dory downed half as much as Drew. Grover spilled the rest. How much juice did Grover spill?

**4.** When a heat wave hit Frostyville, all 12 snowmen suddenly melted. Half were wearing nothing but hats. The rest were wearing hats and gloves. How many gloves hit the ground when the snowmen melted?

### ANSWERS

**1.** 12 stops

**2.** 19 buttons

**3.** Grover spilled $\frac{7}{17}$ of the glass

**4.** 12 gloves

# Make a List, Table, or Chart

This strategy helps us identify and organize what we know. For example, in problems where combinations must be determined, listing all possible combinations is essential to see if students have considered all the possibilities. Setting up tables or charts can also help reveal patterns or relationships that may exist in sets of data.

1. _____
2. _____
3. _____

**MAKE A LIST, TABLE, OR CHART**

## SAMPLE PROBLEM

Peter Pumpernickel is hosting a party to celebrate Sandwich Appreciation Month. The cold-cut platter includes salami, bologna, and pastrami. How many kinds of sandwiches can Peter's guests make?

## Solution

To solve this problem, students should make a systematic list to keep track of all the possible combinations:

1. salami

2. bologna

3. pastrami

4. salami and bologna

5. salami and pastrami

6. salami, bologna, and pastrami

7. bologna and pastrami

**Answer:** 7 possible cold-cut combos

# SAMPLE PROBLEMS

**1.** Smelta Airlines is running a special on tickets to the Dunesville desert. On Sunday, one ticket costs $10.20. On Monday, it goes up to $20.30. On Tuesday, it costs $30.40. If this pattern continues, how much does a ticket cost on Saturday?

**2.** The National Thumb-wrestling League (N.T.L.) has 5 teams: Toledo, Trenton, Tampa, Texarkana, and Toronto. Each team plays the others once per season. How many games are played in an N.T.L. season?

**3.** Ned Noodle runs a delivery service called NedEx. He guarantees next-year delivery. Ned delivered his first package in 1997. He delivered 2 packages in 1998, 4 in 1999, and 8 in 2000. If this pattern continues, how many deliveries will Ned make in 2010?

**4.** Welcome to the first annual Nicecar race! The drivers are Polite Peter, Courteous Cooter, Pleasant Plato, and Sweet Sven. How many different ways could they finish the race?

## ANSWERS

**1.** $70.80

**2.** 10 games

**3.** 8,192 packages

**4.** 24 ways

# Identify Too Much or Too Little Information

**I**n the real world, we sometimes encounter situations in which we have too much or too little information to solve a problem. The same goes in the math world. Often, word problems contain information that isn't needed to find the solutions. In this case, it's best to read the question carefully, then go back and focus on the numbers and facts needed to answer the question. Suggest that students cross out any irrelevant facts and numbers to simplify the word problem, if necessary.

**IDENTIFY TOO MUCH OR TOO LITTLE INFORMATION**

Other times, a problem may be missing key bits of information necessary to solve the problem. While such problems rarely appear on standardized tests, it's good practice for students to learn to identify what information they would need to solve such a problem.

## SAMPLE PROBLEM

Doogie McDougal is whipping up 72 different snacks for his 12th annual Blooper Bowl bash. He invited 138 guests—but only $\frac{1}{6}$ are coming. That doesn't bother Doogie. He still makes 100 bowls of nacho dip. He makes twice as many bowls of chili. How many guests are coming to the party?

### Solution

There is more information than we need to solve this problem. The question is how many guests are coming to Doogie's party. To figure this, we divide 138 by 6 (since $\frac{1}{6}$ of the invited guests plan to attend). **Answer:** 23

# SAMPLE PROBLEMS

**1.** Skinny Skeeter won the celery-eating contest. He set a new record! He finished a piece of celery 15 minutes faster than last year's champ, Wispy Wanda. What information do you need to figure out how long it took Skeeter to finish his celery?

**2.** For dessert, Jen is serving red, white, and blue bananas on a stick. She used 23 ounces of red dye and 47 ounces of blue dye to make the colorful bananas. She has 1,464 leftover napkins, so she wraps 2 napkins around each banana. By the end of the barbecue, all the bananas are gone. Jen's niece, Nelly, made a lovely jewelry box with the used sticks. How many sticks did she use?

**3.** Salvatore the singing waiter sang 2 songs every time he visited Vera's table. Vera ordered 2 appetizers that cost $6.02 a piece. She ordered 17 chicken wings for a total of $8.99. For dessert, Vera had 6 cookies and 3 glasses of milk. Salvatore made 16 trips to her table! How many songs did he sing?

**4.** Ollie's oven mitt sold for $6 more than Ollie's iron at Northeby's Auction House. The auction took place at 7 A.M. and was attended by 6 people (including Ollie.) Each person paid 17 cents to enter. What information do you need to figure out how much Ollie's oven mitt sold for?

## ANSWERS

**1.** How long did it take Wanda to finish last year?

**2.** 732 sticks

**3.** 32 songs

**4.** How much did Ollie's iron sell for?

# Find a Pattern

**U**sing lists and drawing pictures can help reveal patterns that may exist within the information a problem supplies. To discover patterns, ask: What relationships do you see between the numbers in the problem? How far apart are the numbers from each other? Do they increase or decrease by certain amounts in certain ways? Remind students that asking these questions will often lead to a good solution.

```
ABAB
AB?
───────
FIND A PATTERN
```

## SAMPLE PROBLEM

Rusty spent $10 to mail a 10-pound watermelon to his Uncle Louie in Louisville. Rusty's brother Bucky spent $12 to send a 12-pound watermelon. It cost their sister Cindy $14 to send Uncle Louie a 14-pound watermelon. How much did sister Samantha spend to send a 20-pounder to Uncle Louie?

## Solution

Notice how the dollar amounts in this problem match the weights of the watermelons mailed. The pattern shows that it costs a dollar for every pound of watermelon mailed. We can surmise that a 20-pound watermelon would cost $20.
**Answer:** $20

# SAMPLE PROBLEMS

**1.** The Paramus Pigeon pitcher just threw a curveball. Next, he plans to hurl a fastball, followed by a curveball, and another curveball. After that it's fastball, curveball, curveball, fastball. Continuing this pattern, what will he throw after that?

**2.** Superstitious Steve has a special ritual. Every morning he taps his alarm clock twice. Then he yawns once. Next, he taps his clock 3 times, followed by 2 yawns. Then he taps the clock 4 times and yawns 3 times. Following this pattern, how many times does he tap the clock next?

**3.** Limber Lou has an interesting way of getting to work. First, he hops, then he skips, then he does a cartwheel. Then he hops, skips, and does 2 cartwheels. That's followed by a hop, a skip, and 3 cartwheels. If he continues this pattern, what will he do next?

**4.** O X O O X O O O X X X O O O O X X X  What comes next in this pattern?

## ANSWERS

**1.** Curveball

**2.** 5 times

**3.** He hops.

**4.** X

# Use Logical Reasoning

**L**ogical reasoning is a way to help students organize data and use the process of elimination to solve problems. Logic boxes and logic lines (see page 80) are helpful tools for organizing facts and using the process of elimination.

USE LOGICAL REASONING

## SAMPLE PROBLEM 1

Skippy, Steve, and Stanley are on their way to a family reunion. One is traveling by hot-air balloon, another by blimp, and the third by pogo stick. Who's on the pogo stick? Use these clues to figure it out:

• Steve is afraid of blimps.
• Stanley is afraid of pogo sticks.
• Skippy loves balloons.

### Solution

From the clues, we know that Steve won't travel by blimp. Put an X in the logic box next to Steve under Blimp. Stanley is afraid of pogo sticks so put an X next to Stanley under Pogo Stick. Skippy loves balloons so put a check next to Skippy under Balloon, and X out Pogo Stick and Blimp. X out the rest of the Balloon column. If Steve isn't in the balloon or blimp, he must be on the pogo stick. **Answer:** Steve is on the pogo stick.

|  | Blimp | Pogo Stick | Balloon |
|---|---|---|---|
| Steve | ✗ | ✓ | ✗ |
| Stanley | ✓ | ✗ | ✗ |
| Skippy | ✗ | ✗ | ✓ |

## SAMPLE PROBLEM 2

The airplane was invented after the telephone and peanut butter. George Washington Carver invented peanut butter after Alexander Graham Bell gave us the telephone. Which invention came first?

### Solution

To solve, draw a logic line. We know that peanut butter goes to the left of the airplane and that the telephone goes to the left of peanut butter. **Answer:** The telephone was the first to be invented of the three.

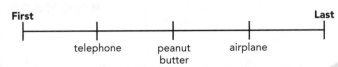

First                    Last

telephone    peanut butter    airplane

$9 + 7 = 16 + 4 = 20 - 7 = 13$

# SAMPLE PROBLEMS

**1.** Emerald Legasping is hosting a dinner party. He's planning to serve the fried watermelon after the pickled peanuts. The clam and cheese sandwiches will be served before the watermelon. The peanuts will come out after the clam and cheese. Which dish will Emerald serve last?

**2.** In the last round of *Reel of Fortune*, Zach has more points than Jason, but less than Jeremy. Who is in the lead?

**3.** Wanda, Warner, and Wilbur are at the Dinky Diner. One ordered a squid sandwich. One ordered a licorice milkshake. And the third ordered fried fish lips. Who ordered what?

Use the clues to find out.
**Clues:**
• Wilbur is allergic to seafood.
• Warner won't eat anything fried.

**4.** Hattie Hatfield is buying gifts for her sons Homer, Hugo, and Beuford. She bought a New Fork Hankees baseball cap, an actual base from the New Fork Hankees baseball stadium, and a chocolate monkey.

Who received what? Use the clues to find out.
**Clues:**
• Beuford hates baseball.
• Hugo is afraid of hats.

### ANSWERS

**1.** Fried watermelon
**2.** Jeremy

**3.** Warner ordered the sandwich, Wilbur ordered the milkshake, and Wanda ordered the fried fish lips.

**4.** Beuford received the monkey, Hugo got the base, and Homer got the cap.

## STRATEGY 8:

# Work Backward

**WORK BACKWARD**

Working backward is a good strategy to use when we know how a problem ends up, but don't know how it started. The trick is to know where to begin and to think about using inverse operations.

## SAMPLE PROBLEM

Donovan Doogle bought a bag of peanuts at the Dingaling Brothers Circus. He feeds half the peanuts to Elwood the elephant. Then he gives 4 peanuts to Marvin the monkey. Donovan eats the last 3 peanuts himself. How many peanuts were in the bag to begin with?

## Solution

• To solve the problem, students can work backward. At the problem's end, Donovan ate 3 peanuts. Before that, he fed Marvin 4 peanuts. That's 3 + 4, or 7 peanuts.

• Before that, Donovan fed Elwood the elephant half of the peanuts. He had 7 peanuts after that, so he must have had twice as many peanuts before. That's 7 x 2, or 14 peanuts. **Answer:** The bag had 14 peanuts in all.

• Have students work forward to check the answer. See if the problem works if Donovan began with 14 peanuts.

$$9 + 7 = 16 + 4 = 20 - 7 = 13$$

# SAMPLE PROBLEMS

**1.** Buddy Buckaroo is competing in an unusual rodeo. He rides an angry armadillo 20 seconds longer than he rides a panicky porcupine. He rides the porcupine 5 times as long as he rides a jumpy jaguar. He stayed on the jaguar for 2 whole seconds! How long did Buddy ride the armadillo?

**2.** Ravenous Roy loves gooey gumdrops. He ate 6 times as many gumdrops from 11 A.M. to 12 P.M. as he did from 10 A.M. to 11 A.M. From 10 A.M. to 11 A.M., he ate half as many gumdrops as he ate from 9 A.M. to 10 A.M. From 9 A.M. to 10 A.M., he ate 10 times as many gumdrops as he ate yesterday. And yesterday's grand total was 12 gumdrops. How many gumdrops did Roy eat today?

**3.** Pedro Pepperoni made a humongous pizza pie. He gave half the slices to his sister Anchovia. He gave 16 slices to his mama, Mia. He gave 12 pieces to his cousin Clifford. And he ate the last 17 slices himself. How many pieces were in the pizza?

**4.** The Walnuts for Walruses charity collected 3 times as many walnuts in June as they did in May. They were given half as many walnuts in May as they were in April. In April, they collected 5 times as many walnuts as they did in March. Their walnut total for March was 500. How many walnuts did they get in June?

## ANSWERS
**1.** 30 seconds
**2.** 540 gumdrops
**3.** 90 slices
**4.** 3,750 walnuts

# The Happy Hundred Word Problems

**T**he "Happy Hundred Word Problems" are organized by the NCTM content standards. Within each standard section, problems are further organized and labeled by the major math concepts typically found in fifth-grade math curriculums. For example, Number and Operations is a large standard that includes concepts like multiplication, division, fractions, and decimals. There are specific word problems here for each of these concepts. The answers are provided in the answer key on pp. 77–79.

As you introduce a problem, remind students to use the Five-Step Process. Keep the graphic organizer prominently displayed on a poster or chart, or give students a copy of their own to refer to. On each page you will find two problems with space for students to show their thinking. Encourage students to write down their solution process including any words, numbers, pictures, diagrams, or tables they use. This helps students with their thinking and understanding of the problem, while giving you more assessment information.

When assessing students' work on word problems, two major aspects need consideration: process and product. Observe students as they work on or discuss problems. Focus on what they say, and whether they use manipulatives, pictures, computation on scrap paper, or other strategies. When looking at their written products consider what skills they are exhibiting as well as what errors or misunderstandings they may be showing. This is why it is essential that students "show their thinking" as they solve a problem and explain their rationale.

Finally, have fun! These problems are designed to appeal to kids' sense of humor. Enjoy the situations and the process. Using what they know to solve word problems gives students a sense of mastery, accomplishment, meaning, and math power!

# NUMBER AND OPERATIONS
## WHOLE NUMBER COMPUTATION

### 1  Whole Number Computation

Professor Frederick Fossilface loves to discover new dinosaurs. He has 5 jars full of dino bones in his lab. Jar A contains 83 bones. Jar B has 79. Jar C has 94 bones. Jar D has 85. And Jar E has 90 bones. The professor clears out 3 jars to build, er, discover, a new dinosaur with 262 bones. Which jars did he use to build the "Fredosaur"?

### 2  Whole Number Computation

Clovus T. Cow teaches tap-dancing to dogs and ducks. He has the same number of each in his class. If he ordered 45 pairs of tap shoes, how many dogs and how many ducks are in his tap-dance class?

**3**  Whole Number Computation

Chef Jeff is baking 7 special cupcakes for Skippy, his pet seal. He wants to place 1 red fish and 3 blue fish on each cupcake. How many fish does Jeff need?

**4** Whole Number Computation

Chef Jeff baked 700 clam cookies for Miss Bliss's class. There are 35 kids in the class. Miss Bliss would like to give each student the same number of cookies and have none leftover. Can she?

**5** Whole Number Computation

Hank has 600 bowling cards in his collection. He gives 16 cards to his friend Phil, 41 to his sister Frieda, and 37 to his great grandma Gladys. How many cards did Hank give away?

**6** Whole Number Computation

Chet had 1,000,000 chestnuts stored up for winter — and they're all gone! (Chet's not a squirrel, he just loves chestnuts.) Chad ate 200,000 more than Chet. But Chet ate 100,000 more than Chip. How many chestnuts did Chet eat?

**7** Whole Number Computation

Maria bought one T-shirt for each of her friends. She bought 3 blue shirts, 18 yellow shirts, 42 green shirts, and 62 orange shirts. The rest were purple. What information do you need to figure out how many purple shirts Maria bought?

**8** Whole Number Computation

Singing in the Drain

Harold has 100 tickets to the new show *Singing in the Drain*. He gives 12 to his sister Maude and 27 to his brother Claude. Harold is saving the rest for his favorite cousin Clara. How many tickets does he have for his cousin Clara?

## 9    Whole Number Computation

In 2005, Norman knitted 13 more sweaters than he did the year before. In 2003, he knitted 12 sweaters. That's 23 fewer than his total for 2004. How many sweaters did Norman knit from 2003 through 2005?

## 10    Whole Number Computation

Kimmy loves to watch reruns of the TV show *Mr. Odd*. Each episode is 26 minutes long. That's 2 minutes longer than Kimmy's other favorite show, *The Golden Gargoyles*. Last week the Sickelodeon network showed *Mr. Odd* 4 times a day, 5 days a week. It showed *The Golden Gargoyles* half as many times, but over 6 days. Kimmy didn't miss a minute of *Mr. Odd* last week. How much time did she spend watching the show last week?

**11** Whole Number Computation

Sally the seamstress specializes in sweaters for sea creatures. She just filled two big orders, one for O.O.O. (Organization of Octopi) and the other for U.F.E. (United Federation of Eels). Each group ordered the same number of sweaters. If there were a total of 312 sleeves, how many sweaters did Sally make? (Hint: How many "arms" does each animal have?)

**12** Whole Number Computation

It took Milo and Myron 330 hours to fly their saucer from Mars to Earth. Milo piloted the saucer 21 times longer than Myron did. How long did Myron fly the ship?

**13** | Whole Number Computation

Sammy sees 72 seals off the shore at 7:05 P.M. Each seal weighs more than 200 pounds! He feeds each seal 3 fish. Later, twice as many sea lions show up. The biggest one weighs more than 1,000 pounds. Sammy gives each of the sea lions one fish. If he has 5 fish left, how many did he start with?

**14** | Whole Number Computation

The Huntsville Howlers hockey team set a new record! They scored twice as many goals in the first period as in the second period. They scored 5 more goals in the second period than in the third period. And in the third period, they scored $\frac{1}{8}$ as many goals as they scored in overtime. In overtime, the Howlers found the net 72 times! How many goals did they score in all?

## 15    Whole Number Computation

Byron the bookworm is burrowing his way through a copy of *The Lizard of Roz*. He chews through the first 17 pages on Monday. He gnaws through 5 times as many on Tuesday. And he eats through to the last page on Wednesday. What information do you need to figure out how many pages Byron burrows through on Wednesday?

## 16    Whole Number Computation

Magico the Magician has a set of kooky cards: 3 cards show squirrels playing chess, 2 cards show a monkey reading a newspaper, 5 cards show bunnies bowling, and 10 cards show a skateboarding duck. What are the chances of Magico pulling a card with a duck on it?

**17** Whole Number Computation

Puddles, Pancho's pet poodle, spent the day at doggy day-care and came home with fleas. 600 fleas jumped off Puddles during dinner. 760 fleas jumped off while Puddles played fetch. 375 fleas fled when Puddles got his nightly bath. And the final 4 fleas jumped off when Puddles brushed his teeth. How many fleas did Puddles come home with?

**18** Whole Number Computation

Hester and Chester Cheapskate plan to spend exactly $50 on new living-room furniture at Jerry's Junk Joint. Hester likes the $15 plastic couch, the $10 cardboard chair, and the $5 coffee table made of coffee cans. Chester loves the $20 Styrofoam chair and the $15 TV stand made of broken TVs. They spend the whole $50 on three different items. Which items did they buy?

**19**    **Whole Number Computation**

It's Edwina's 10th birthday. Her mother is lighting the candles on the cake. There is a candle for each year plus one for every guest at the party, plus Edwina and her mom. In all, 137 guests were invited to the party. How many candles are on the cake?

**20**    **Whole Number Computation**

Buster the bull just ran into a china shop! He busts 60 platters into 7,000 pieces. He breaks half as many $65 vases, and 3 times as many $400 plates as platters. The pile of pieces is 30 feet high! How many plates did Buster bust?

## 21 Whole Number Computation

Generous Gina is very, well, generous. In January she donated a jar of gumballs to charity. She plans to double the size of her donation every month until the end of the year! How many jars of gumballs will she donate in the year?

## 22 Whole Number Computation

The Norville Leadenbocker popcorn company is buying back all of the defective kernels they've sold over the years. They are paying one penny per kernel. Norville figures they sell one million duds per year. What information do you need to figure out how much the big kernel buy-back will cost the company?

**Whole Number Computation**

In yesterday's game against the Chicago Shlubs, New York Hankees' second baseman Alfoonzi Sorrymano made 5 more errors than the third baseman, Darren Goon. Goon made 10 more errors than the shortstop, Eric Meathead. Meathead had a total of 10 errors in the game. How many mistakes did Sorrymano make?

Darren Goon

**24** **Whole Number Computation**

The ants are building a new hill. When it's done, it'll be 6 inches tall! They are adding 7,955,002 grains of sand per day. That makes one inch of height for the hill. Will the finished hill require more or less than 48,000,0000 grains of sand?

## 25 Whole Number Computation

Mildred Moneybags started the day with $100,000 in her purse (it's a big purse). Then she went on quite the shopping spree. First she bought an antique paperweight for $23,000. Then she picked up a $50,000 first-edition of her favorite book, *A Tale of Two Suburbs*. She also bought a $13,500 porcelain pig. How much did Mildred spend today?

## 26 Whole Number Computation

Mervin Hosslebock didn't become a yodeling sensation overnight. He started taking yodeling lessons in 1923 when he was 6 years old. He practiced every day until he got his big break—when he was asked to join the chart-topping group, the Yodel-ay-hee-hoos. It happened on his 82nd birthday! On what year did Mervin get his big break?

**Fractions and Decimals**

The Tremain triplets—Troy, Travis, and Tricia—recently ran in the Manitoba mini-marathon. Together, they ran a total of $6\frac{1}{2}$ hours. Each one ran exactly the same amount of time. How long did each triplet run?

**28**   **Fractions and Decimals**

The Grady's rose garden is 15.75 feet long. The Gordon's rose garden is 32 times longer than the Grady's. How long is the Gordon's rose garden?

Math Word Problems Made Easy: Grade 5   Scholastic Teaching Resources

**Fractions and Decimals**

Stewie studied for a math test for 26 hours. Stevie studied $\frac{1}{4}$ as long. How long did Stevie study?

**Fractions and Decimals**

Baseball coach Moe Glory selected 3 players for the all-star team. Erik Skeeter earns $38,500.52 per game. Mason Salami makes $49,333.13 a game, while Randy Petrock earns $28,749.35. Roger Lemons makes $62,010.62 and David Smells gets $21,000.29 per game. Together, Moe's choices make $116,583 per game. Which 3 players made the all-star team?

**Fractions and Decimals**

Murphy has 50 marbles. Morty has half as many marbles as Murphy. And Millie has $\frac{1}{5}$ as many marbles as Morty. How many marbles do they have all together?

**Fractions and Decimals**

Sid's been stranded on a desert island for six months. Fortunately for him, food keeps washing up on shore. A box with 100 bagels washed up first. Half as many apples washed up after that. A shipment of pickles appeared the next day. There were 4.2 times as many pickles as apples. How many pickles did Sid get?

**Fractions and Decimals**

Tony took a taxi from Dizzy World to Tea World. The driver changed lanes every 12.5 miles. The trip was a total of 112.5 miles. How many times did the driver change lanes?

**Fractions and Decimals**

Craig's crayon company made 400 green crayons today! That's $\frac{1}{4}$ the number of red crayons. How many red crayons did Craig's company make today?

**35** Fractions and Decimals

Rover ran from the vet's office to his dog house in 4 minutes. It took Roger (Rover's owner) 7.5 times as long to run the same distance. How long did it take Roger to get to Rover's house?

**36** Fractions and Decimals

Alvin the shoe salesman sold 8 pairs of shoes before lunch. Half of the shoes he sold cost $72 a pair, $\frac{1}{4}$ cost $32.50 a pair, and the rest are 50 percent off the original price of $64.80. How much did the 8 pairs of shoes cost all together?

**37** Fractions and Decimals

For Valentine's Day, Luigi Loomis bought his sweetie, Svetlana, some very special gifts. He paid $6.99 each for three paperbacks, *The Mediocre Gatsby*, *Boysenberry Finn*, and *Catcher in the Ryebread*. He bought her an autographed copy of The Bedbugs new CD, *I Wanna Hold Your Hat* for $\frac{1}{3}$ of what he paid for all the books. How much did Luigi spend on Svetlana's presents?

**38** Fractions and Decimals

Vito bought 3 violins for $30.07 apiece. His brother Harry bought 32 harmonicas for $17.05 each. Their sister Sally bought one violin from Vito for $32 and one harmonica from Harry for $10.07. Sally sold the violin for $73.50 and gave the harmonica to charity. How much profit did Vito make when he sold a violin to Sally?

**Fractions and Decimals**

Mac, Milo, Moose, and Myrna are mice. Mac ate 6,480,000 pieces of cheese last year. Moose ate $\frac{6}{18}$ of that amount. Myrna ate $\frac{5}{24}$ . And Milo polished off $\frac{16}{32}$ of Mac's total. Who ate the least cheese last year?

**Fractions and Decimals**

Yolanda used 15.6 feet of fabric to make a fabulous new dress. That's 3 times the length of fabric she used for her new hat. How many feet of fabric did Yolanda use for her hat?

46  *Math Word Problems Made Easy:*
**Grade 5**

**41**    **Fractions and Decimals**

Cindy is making her special olive-pineapple soup. The recipe calls for 64 black olives, 4.5 times as many green olives, and 41.5 pounds of pineapple. She cooks half of the pineapple in a pot of water. The she adds 31 black olives and lets it cook twice as long. Afterwards she pours in all of the green olives. How many green olives are in the soup?

**42**    **Fractions and Decimals**

The Quentin quintuplets are buying a used lawnmower for their father, Quincy. Sandy's piggy bank has $5.27 inside. Andy's has $.32. Randy's has $16.01. Iggy's has $12.99. And Herbie's bank contains $.49. One of the kids forgot to bring his piggy bank to the store, so they bought a lawnmower for $22.09. Who forgot his bank?

### 43     Fractions and Decimals

Otis, the elevator operator, makes $97.52 per hour. (He works in a very fancy elevator.) He earned 4 times as much on Monday than he earned on Tuesday. And he earned $\frac{1}{8}$ as much on Tuesday than he did Wednesday. On Wednesday, Otis earned $780.16. How many hours did Otis work on Monday?

### 44     Fractions and Decimals

Carrie just loves the merry-go-round. She's been on it for 17 hours straight! That's 2.5 times her old record! How many hours was Carrie's old record?

## 45 Fractions and Decimals

Mighty Minnie won a weight-lifting contest. She lifted $161\frac{1}{2}$ pounds more than Burly Betty. Betty hoisted $\frac{1}{3}$ of the weight lifted by Mildred Muscles. And Mildred lifted 5 kindergartners. Each one weighed 48 pounds! How much weight did Minnie lift?

## 46 Fractions and Decimals

Evelyn and Elrod invited 777 guests to their wedding. They all showed up, but only $\frac{1}{7}$ brought gifts. How many guests brought a gift for Evelyn and Elrod?

**47** Fractions and Decimals

Mason hit a 375.5-foot home run with a 2-pound bat. 100-pound Arnie smacked a 325-foot home run with a 2.5-pound bat. Stella weighs just 98 pounds, but she walloped a baseball with a 3-pound bat and it flew 456.2 feet for a grand-slam home run! How much longer was Stella's home run than Mason's?

**48** Fractions and Decimals

Polly is filling her pool with pudding for her pet panda, Paulie. Paulie eats 1,800 ounces of pudding a day! Polly pays $20 for 35 giant pudding packets and empties them into the pool. Polly pours 25 gallons of water and 25 gallons of milk into the pool to make 6,517.25 ounces of pudding! How much will be left after Paulie finishes eating today?

**49** Fractions and Decimals

Little Lenny is very proud of his sock collection. He has 10 more blue socks than red socks and $\frac{1}{2}$ as many green socks as red socks. He has 6 fewer holey socks than striped socks and 12 more green socks than striped socks. He's wearing his two holey socks right now! How many socks does Lenny have?

**50** Fractions and Decimals

Bucky pays 30¢ per minute for his cell-phone calls. He spent 6.5 hours on his cell phone blabbing about Becky's bad report card. He spent 7 hours and 31 minutes gossiping about Gabe's bad haircut. And he called his cousin Carlotta to complain about her cooking. The call to Carlotta cost $17.40! How much did the calls cost all together?

**51**   Fractions and Decimals

Percy Pucker has whipped up a very special batch of lemonade—it's just lemon juice and water. He promises half the pitcher to his friend Louie. Lena can have half as much as of what Louie gets. Lyle gets a quarter of Lena's portion. And the rest goes to Ralph. How much does Ralph get?

**52**   Fractions and Decimals

Great Grandma Gooseberry is having a bake sale. She sold her pies by the slice. Each pie had 8 slices. A slice of gooseberry pie costs $2.75. A slice of blueberry pie goes for $3.50. Huckleberry pies are 2 slices for $5. In the first hour she had sold 10 slices of gooseberry pie, 28 slices of blueberry pie, and 5 slices of huckleberry pies. How much money did she make in the first hour?

**53** Fractions and Decimals

Jojo went to Seaweed World and won a contest for guessing Milford the Manatee's weight! He spent $\frac{1}{2}$ of the prize money on presents for Milford. He spent $\frac{1}{2}$ as much buying presents for his brother J.J. as for Milford. That was the same amount he spent on himself. He bought himself one present: 20 shirts at his favorite store, the Buck Bin (where everything's a dollar). After that, he was out of money. How much did Jojo win in the contest?

**54** Fractions and Decimals

Coco is cooking a casserole. She uses $\frac{1}{5}$ as many beets as she does plums, and 100 times as many beets as she does anchovies. She used 10.5 anchovies. How many plums are in the casserole?

**55** Algebra

Princess Priscilla wants to look spectacular for the palace bowling tournament. She has 4 bowling shirts to choose from (red, blue, green, and plaid), and 5 different crowns (gold, silver, diamond, emerald, and ruby). How many different combinations of one shirt and one crown can she make?

**56** Algebra

Barney is replacing a burnt-out bulb on his Christmas tree. He notices that the string has lights in this order: red, white, green, blue, red, white, green, blue, red, white, green, blue, etc. The burnt bulb is the 17th in the strand. What color should it be?

## 57 Algebra

Doctor Piper has invented the perfect soft drink. The problem? He can't remember the three main ingredients! In his lab he has cinnamon, sugar, pepperoni, and petunia petals. How many combinations of these ingredients might be the secret recipe?

## 58 Algebra

*Star Bores XVII: Attack of the Clowns* made $100,000,000 on opening day! It made $80,000,000 on day 2 of its release. On day 3, it made $60,000,000. If this pattern continues, how much will it make on day 4?

**59** Algebra

The Days Out Motel has a strange pricing system. On the 1st of each month, a room costs $44 a night. On the 2nd day of the month, the price goes up $6. It goes up another $6 on the 3rd of the month, and so on. How much is a room at the Days Out Motel on the 16th day of the month?

**60** Algebra

Spiffy Poop popcorn isn't very good. Only 2 out of every 5 kernels actually pop. How many kernels must you have to make 20 popped pieces of Spiffy Poop popcorn?

**61** Algebra

Red, yellow, green, red, blue, blue,
blue, red, yellow, green, red, blue,
blue, blue, red, yellow, green . . .
What color comes next in this pattern?

**62** Algebra

Lenny, Benny, Jenny, and Penny
worked together to build the
world's biggest birdhouse. It's
700 feet tall! Lenny spent 18
hours on the project. Penny spent
twice as long as Lenny. Benny
worked a third as long as Penny,
but 6 times longer than Jenny.
How many hours did Jenny work
on the birdhouse?

 **63** Algebra

Just once, Niles Stiles would like to beat his brother Giles in a race. It takes Giles just 3 hours to run 2 miles! Niles practices every month. In October he ran 2 miles in 1,074 minutes. In November he did it in 895 minutes. And in December he did it in 716 minutes. If he keeps improving at this rate, in what month will Niles beat Giles?

**64** Algebra

Birthday boy Benny made a pyramid of presents. He put 50 presents on the top level, 100 on the level below that, and 150 on the one below that. His pyramid has 5 levels. If Benny continued this pattern, how many presents did he get in all for his birthday?

## 65    Algebra

Poor Percy Pauper has just 27 cents in his purse. How many different coin combinations could he have? (Hint: List all the combinations to help you keep track.)

## 66    Algebra

Predictable Pete isn't a very good quarterback. He only knows three plays: pass the ball, punt the ball, call time out. On the first 8 plays he passed, punted, called time, called time, passed, punted, called time, and called time. If he keeps up this pattern, what will he do on the 41st play of the game?

**67** Algebra

It's Saturday, and the ants are marching 2 by 2 (hurrah, hurrah!). They plan to march 4 by 4 on Sunday and 16 by 16 on Monday. How will they be marching on Wednesday?

**68** Algebra

Get ready for the Battle of the Bands! The Rotten Apples, Skinny Screamers, and Loud Losers are all performing at Bubba Bruiser's Bandshell. How many different ways can Bubba set the performance line-up?

### 69    Algebra

Baseball pitcher Ollie Toes just threw a spitball. He follows that with a slider. Next comes a curveball, followed by a fastball, spitball, slider, curveball, fastball, and another spitball. Continuing this pattern, what will he throw next?

Ollie Toes

### 70    Algebra

Daisy May Dooley started teaching banjo lessons when she was 32 years old. She had 15 kids in her class that year. The following year, Daisy had 17 kids in her banjo class. When she was 34, she had a class of 19 kids. The next year, her class size grew to 21. This year, she has 41 kids in her class. If she continued this pattern, how old is Daisy May now?

### **71**   Algebra

The Paramus Pigeons' pitcher is very superstitious. He pats his head 5 times in the first inning of every game. In the second inning, he pats his head 7 times. In the third, he pats his head 9 times. How many times does the pitcher pat his head in the 9th inning?

### **72**   Algebra

On Monday, Grover the grocer sells fresh garbanzo beans for $4.25 a pound. On Tuesday, he sells them for $4 per pound. On Wednesday, garbanzos cost $3.75 a pound. If this pattern continues, how much will one pound of garbanzo beans cost on Friday?

## 73 Algebra

Massive Mickey is trying out the new fad diet, the Bone. Mickey loses 2.1 pounds the first week of the diet. He drops 1.8 pounds the second week. In the third week of the diet, Mickey loses 1.5 pounds. If this pattern continues, how much can he expect to lose in week 6 of the Bone diet?

## 74 Algebra

Nelly Nutjob is building a fence around her lawn to keep her neighbors from stepping on her prize-winning dandelions. Instead of wood planks, Nelly is using lava lamps, lawn chairs, and pink flamingoes to make the fence. If she uses the pattern lamp, chair, flamingo, lamp, chair, flamingo . . . what will the 30th piece of the fence be?

 **Algebra**

Sara Stiletto has a special shed for her shoes. It's shaped like the heel of her favorite clog! The floor is covered with 13 rows of shoes (13 is her shoe size!). If there are 272 shoes in the 13$^{th}$ row, 260 in the 12$^{th}$ row, and 248 in the 11$^{th}$ row, how many shoes are in the 2$^{nd}$ row?

 **Geometry and Measurement**

Tiny Tommy likes to keep his huge Captain Carl comic-book collection under his bed. Each comic book is 3 inches thick. His bed is 3 feet, 9 inches high. How many comic books can fit under Tommy's bed?

**77**

### Geometry and Measurement

EMPIRE STATE BUILDING

Superman can leap tall buildings in a single bound, but Super Murray needs a rocket booster. He can leap 3 stories for every 256 ounces* of rocket fuel. The Empire State Building is 102 stories high. How many gallons of rocket fuel does Super Murray need to leap over it?

* 32 ounces = 1 quart; 4 quarts = 1 gallon

**78**

### Geometry and Measurement

Len and Sherry's Ice Cream shop is giving away free ice cream until 5 P.M.! The second Stanley hears the news at 4:10 P.M., he starts to run to the store. It takes him 10 minutes to get down the stairs of his apartment (he lives on the 82nd floor). And it takes him another 45 minutes to run the mile to the store. (Stanley is not a very fast runner.) Does Stanley make it in time to get free ice cream?

**79** Geometry and Measurement

Benny has 57 beans. He plans to drop one bean every 1,056 feet for 2 miles*. How many beans does he drop in 2 miles?

* 1 mile = 5,280 feet

**80** Geometry and Measurement

Tiny Terrence is growing very quickly. He grew half as much in July as he grew in August. He grew 2 times as much in August as he grew in September, when he grew 3 times as much as he grew in October. And in October, he grew an inch. How many centimeters* did Terrence grow from July through October?

* 2.54 centimeters = 1 inch

**81** Geometry and Measurement

Oliver is cutting an old napkin into teeny blankets for his pet mice. The napkin is 5 square inches. How many 1-square-inch blankets can he make?

**82** Geometry and Measurement

Lola, the lawnmower lady, has miles to mow before she sleeps. She starts at 9 A.M. and rides her mower at a steady rate of 15 miles per hour. It'll take her 17 hours to finish mowing the field at Stunway Park. How many miles must be mowed?

### Geometry and Measurement

Lulu the librarian has 6 books to put on a shelf. One-third of the books are each 4 inches thick and $\frac{2}{3}$ of the books are each 2 inches thick. Will all 6 books fit on a shelf that is one-foot wide? Why?

### Geometry and Measurement

It's the first snow of the season, and more than 3 feet fell overnight! Savion has the monumental task of shoveling the driveway, which is 36 feet long and 18 feet wide. What is the area of the rectangular driveway?

**85** Geometry and Measurement

Edith's eyelashes are 11 times shorter than Neville's nose hairs. Neville's nose hairs are 143 inches long. How long are Edith's eyelashes in feet and inches?

**86** Geometry and Measurement

The New Fork Dangers hockey team is sick of playing on ice. It's too cold! They decide to cover their 100-foot-by-80-foot rink with nice warm blankets. Each square blanket has a perimeter of 16 feet. Will 300 blankets cover the whole rink?

## 87   Geometry and Measurement

Wendy adds 3 feet of foil to her giant foil ball every week. She adds 6 feet, 2 inches of string to her ball of string every month. And she adds 13 inches of rubber bands to her rubber-band ball every day. How many feet of string would Wendy have added to her ball of string at the end of 12 months?

## 88   Reasoning

The Bottles are breaking up! That's right, after 68 years of touring, Don, Saul, Sarge, and Wingo are moving on to bigger and better things. One will open a used-sock store. Another will drive an ice-cream truck. One will run for president. And the fourth will manage the New York Hankees dominoes team. Who will do what? Use these clues to find out:
• Wingo never learned how to drive.
• Saul will sell socks or run for president.
• Don is getting ready to campaign in Ohio.

**89** Reasoning

Bet you didn't know Christopher Columbus's distant cousin Skippy discovered Detroit. He also discovered San Francisco, St. Louis, and Secaucus, New Jersey. He discovered all of them during a road trip in 1997. (We never said he was the first to discover them!) He found San Francisco before St. Louis, but after Secaucus. He discovered Detroit after Secaucus, but before San Francisco. Which city did he discover second?

**90** Reasoning

Minnie is taller than Myrna. Myrna is taller than Missy. Millie is taller than Myrna and Minnie. Who is the shortest?

**91** | **Reasoning**

Walter is older than Weezer. Wanda is younger than Weezer. Winnie is older than Weezer, but younger than Walter. Who is the oldest?

**92** | **Reasoning**

Amateur astronomer Nicholas Copernigoose has discovered a new solar system! He named all five planets after friends. Planet Marge is closer to the sun than Stella, but farther than Planet Jack. Jack is farther than Frank, but closer than Irene. Irene is the middle planet. Name the planets in order of distance from the sun.

**93**   **Reasoning**

Brittley Sneers, Brat Fitt, and Sillery Puff are all writing children's books. One is working on *The Three Incredibly Gigantic Pigs.* Another is penning *Larry Rotter and the Goblet of Goop.* The third is finishing up *The Rat in the Vat.* Who's writing what? Use these clues to find out:

• Brat isn't writing about pigs.
• Brittley and Brat are both writing about animals.

**94**   **Reasoning**

The Mighty Mosquitoes finished the baseball season with more wins than the Scary Skeletons, but fewer than the Goofy Goats. The Sinking Sliders won fewer than the Hairy Hoppers, but more than the Goats. Which team won the most games in the season?

## 95    Reasoning

The Tunaville Talent Show is about to begin! Percy the Plate Spinner will perform before Sword-Swallower Sal. Peppy's Prancing Poodles will perform before Percy, but after Lip-syncing Larry. In what order will the audience see the talented acts?

## 96    Reasoning

Fred, Ned, and Ted have made New Year's resolutions. One resolved to eat more ravioli. Another resolved to become an Olympic diver. And the third resolved to call his brother, Ed, on his birthday. Who resolved what? Use these clues and a logic box to solve:

• Fred and Ted are only children.
• Ted is allergic to ravioli.

**97** Reasoning

Terry, Tony, and Tina got temporary tattoos. One got a red flower, one got a blue flower, and one got a red apple. Who got what? Use these clues to solve:
• Tony didn't get a blue tattoo.
• Terry didn't get a flower tattoo.

**98** Reasoning

The Blue Jersey Doubloons just won the Stanley Cupcake! The puck bounced off 4 players before it went into the goal. It hit Scoot Stevens before Spott Gomez, but after Colin Bite. It hit Bite after it bounced off Jett Freezin. The last player to touch the puck got credit for the goal. Who was it?

**Reasoning**

The Mudville Mudpies have a new batting line-up. Mighty Macy bats before Mighty Lacy, but after Mighty Pacy. Mighty Stacey bats before Mighty Macy, but after Mighty Pacy. What is the Mudpie's new batting line-up?

**Reasoning**

Alvin, Calvin, and Moe got new hairdos! One got a perm, one got a buzz cut, and one got a puppy cut. Who got what? Use these clues and a logic box to solve:

• Calvin hates curls.
• Moe is a mutt.

## Number and Operations

### Whole Number Computation

1. Jars A, C, and D

2. 15 dogs and 15 ducks

3. 28 fish

4. Yes

5. 94 cards

6. 300,000 chestnuts

7. We need to know how many friends Maria has.

8. 61 tickets

9. 95 sweaters

10. 8 hours, 40 minutes

11. 78 sweaters

12. 15 hours

13. 365 fish

14. 123 goals

15. We need to know the number of pages in the book.

16. 1 in 2, or 50% chance

17. 1,739 fleas

18. The $15 couch, the $15 TV, and the $20 Styrofoam chair

19. 149 candles

20. 180 plates

21. 4,095 jars of gumballs

22. We need to know how many years the company has been selling popcorn.

23. 25 errors

24. Less than 48,000,000 grains of sand

25. $86,500

26. 1999

### Fractions and Decimals

27. 2 hours, 10 minutes

28. 504 feet long

29. $6\frac{1}{2}$ hours

30. Skeeter, Salami, and Petrock

31. 80 marbles

32. 210 pickles

33. 9 times

34. 1,600 red crayons

35. 30 minutes

36. $417.80

37. $27.96

38. $1.93 profit

39. Myrna

40. 5.2 feet

41. 288 green olives

42. Iggy

43. 4 hours

44. 6.8 hours

45. $241\frac{1}{2}$ pounds

46. 111 guests

47. 80.7 feet longer

48. 4,717.25 ounces of pudding

49. 120 socks

50. $269.70

51. $\frac{3}{16}$ of the pitcher

52. $138

53. $80

54. 5,250 plums

## Algebra

55. 20 combinations

56. Red

57. 4 combinations

58. $40,000,000

59. $134

60. 50 kernels

61. Red

62. 2 hours

63. March

64. 750 presents

65. 13 different combinations

66. Pass the ball

67. 65,536 by 65,536

68. 6 different ways

69. A slider

70. 45 years old

71. 21 times

72. $3.25

73. 0.6 pounds

74. A flamingo

75. 140 shoes

## Geometry and Measurement

76. 15 comic books

77. 68 gallons

78. No

79. 10 beans

80. 33.02 centimeters

81. 25 blankets

82. 255 miles

83. No. The books measure 16 inches thick all together.

84. 648 square feet

85. 1 foot, 1 inch

86. No

87. 74 feet

## Reasoning

88. Don will run for president, Saul will open a sock store, Sarge will drive an ice-cream truck, and Wingo will manage the Hankees.

89. Detroit

90. Missy

91. Walter

92. Frank, Jack, Irene, Marge, Stella

93. Brittley is writing *The Three Incredibly Gigantic Pigs*, Brat is writing *The Rat in the Vat*, and Sillery is writing *Larry Rotter and the Goblet of Goop*.

# ANSWER KEY

**94.** The Hairy Hoppers

**95.** Lip-syncing Larry, Peppy's Prancing Poodles, Percy the Plate Spinner, and Sword-Swallower Sal

**96.** Fred resolved to eat more ravioli, Ted resolved to become a diver, and Ned resolved to call his brother.

**97.** Terry got a red apple, Tony got a red flower, and Tina got a blue flower.

**98.** Spott Gomez

**99.** Mighty Pacy, Mighty Stacey, Mighty Macy, and Mighty Lacy

**100.** Alvin got a perm, Calvin got a buzz cut, and Moe got the puppy cut.

# LOGIC BOX

|  |  |  |  |  |
|--|--|--|--|--|
|  |  |  |  |  |
|  |  |  |  |  |
|  |  |  |  |  |
|  |  |  |  |  |
|  |  |  |  |  |

# LOGIC LINE

*Math Word Problems Made Easy:*
**Grade 5**